MW01244647

A BLONDIE READER

Old Wine in New Verses

James R. Wachob

authorHOUSE®

AuthorHouse™
1663 Liberty Drive
Bloomington, IN 47403
www.authorhouse.com
Phone: 1-800-839-8640

First published by AuthorHouse 5/13/2009

ISBN: 978-1-4389-7180-3 (sc)

Library of Congress Control Number: 2009903108

Printed in the United States of America
Bloomington, Indiana

This book is printed on acid-free paper.

BLONDIE AND ACCIDENT REDUCTION

The cops declared her skills impaired;
she needed more instruction.
With some remorse she found a course
in Accident Reduction.

She paid her fee but proved to be
a victim of deception.
She learned one day to her dismay
it dealt with contraception.

BLONDIE AND DAYLIGHT SAVING TIME

Blondie's scared of global warming;

polar ice will swamp our shore.

Congress, which she says was reckless,

gave us sunshine one hour more!

BLONDIE AND GAS PRICES

Though others gripe that prices soar,

my costs don't ever climb.

As I drive up, I give the man

just twenty bucks each time.

3

BLONDIE AND PORNOGRAPHY

Blondie spurned pornography;

the offers made her laugh:

"What could I appreciate

without a pornograph?"

BLONDIE AND SIGN LANGUAGE

She's taking a sign-language course with the hope

she'll later be able to find

a job that will put her new talents to work:

to teach at a school for the blind.

BLONDIE AND TECH SUPPORT

She sat at her computer
on a dark and stormy night.
Her monitor stopped working,
and it gave her quite a fright.

She couldn't keep on surfing,
so she phoned to Tech Support:
"Just now I got a problem
of a very crazy sort."

"Please read the model number,"
said the techie loud and clear.
"I can't," said Blondie sadly,
"there's a power outage here."

BLONDIE AND THE BARKING DOG

The neighbors' dog barked loud and long,
a tiresome nuisance nightly.
So Blondie left the couple's bed,
went out, returning sprightly.

"I fixed the problem," Blondie said,
while cagily explaining:
"I moved the dog to OUR backyard;
now THEY can start complaining!"

BLONDIE AND THE BIOLOGY TEST

"What birds," was the question, "give others their young?

The answer goes into the box."

So Blondie wrote "cuckoos," explaining her choice:

"No room for the young in the clocks."

BLONDIE AND THE BIRD

While strolling with Blondie one day in the park,

a friend cried: "Poor birdie! It's dead!"

But Blondie, not thinking to look on their path,

was searching the heavens instead.

BLONDIE AND THE BLOOD TEST

She's cramming so she won't appear

to be a blonde buffoon.

She wants to know the answers for

her blood test scheduled soon.

BLONDIE AND THE BOMB THREAT

Blondie has heard there are bombs that are "dirty,"

whose fallout can stifle computers with ease.

Fearful, she wonders if bombing her building

would cause the erasure of all her CD's.

BLONDIE AND THE CAR REPAIR

When her car was badly dented
and she planned for its repair,
then a neighbor said, "Save money,
you can do the job with air.

"Put your lips around the tailpipe,
and you blow until you're blue.
All the dents will pop out quickly,
and your car will look like new."

When the neighbor saw no progress,
he unfairly asked her why.
"I forgot to close the windows,"
said dear Blondie in reply.

BLONDIE AND THE CRASH COURSE

"You need to take a crash course now,"

her patient teacher said.

So Blondie took those words to heart

and started Drivers Ed.

BLONDIE AND THE DINOSAUR PARK

She went to a dinosaur theme park one day,

robotics of cinema grade.

Disheartened, she asked for a refund and said:

"A couple were fake, I'm afraid."

BLONDIE AND THE DOG FOOD

She had a lot of dogs around,
some black, some white, same breed.
She wondered why it always was
that blacks cost more to feed.

She called a vet to visit her,
who urged her to relax.
He smiled and said, "It's simple, ma'am,
you've twice as many blacks."

BLONDIE AND THE DRESS CODE

The girls in the classroom were scantily clad
and thought it was perfectly "cool."
Describing them Jezebels luring the boys,
the teacher made long sleeves the rule.

But Blondie liked T-shirts and wore them a lot;
she wanted to show off her charms.
Defying the teacher, she wouldn't obey
and cited "the right to bare arms."

BLONDIE AND THE DRUGSTORE SCALES

When Blondie wondered what she weighed,

she quickly spent a dime.

Unhappily she read the words:

"Just one, please, at a time."

BLONDIE AND THE EXERCISE PROGRAM

"Exercise gives added years!"

The thought was very heady.

Blondie, starting, said, "It's true;

I've aged ten years already."

BLONDIE THE CUB REPORTER

The editor, angry, took Blondie to task:
"So where's your report for today?
The mayor was married at noon, as you know.
Now why the outrageous delay?"

"There's really no story," said Blondie unfazed,
"it's perfectly simple, you see.
I'll tell you what happened at twelve in the church
and think that you'll surely agree.

"The couple was standing in front of the priest
when someone insulted the bride.
The mayor turned 'round and unholstered his gun
and shot while the womenfolk cried.

"The murder caused chaos, the candles fell down,
the altar cloth quickly caught fire.
The priest went unconscious inhaling the smoke;
the flaming reached up to the choir.

"And now," added Blondie, "you know what I knew
in making my best judgment call.
No sense in pretending the wedding took place.
There wasn't a story at all!"

BLONDIE AND THE GUN

When Blondie found her man in bed,
a sweetie by his side,
she drew a pistol from her purse
to show her wounded pride.

"I'll kill myself in front of you,"
said Blondie clearly vexed.
The man cried, "NO," but she replied,
"Shut up or you'll be next."

BLONDIE AND THE JIGSAW PUZZLE

She finished the puzzle in 17 months,

concluding a long stretch of tears.

She's proud she succeeded in winning the race;

the label said "3 to 5 years."

BLONDIE AND THE LOTTERY

She cried herself to sleep each night;
her case seemed kind of funny.
She often guessed the numbers right
but never got the money.

She raised her problem up to God
and prayed for help to lick it.
A patient voice said, "Blondie dear,
you've got to buy a ticket!"

BLONDIE AND THE NEW BUS

She waited in vain for her Bus 44
but saw then a Bus 22.
Exhausted from standing, she welcomed a ride
and felt that the new bus would do.

She boarded the bus she knew nothing about,
and frankly she hadn't a care.
She thought she'd get home on the Bus 22
by doubling the regular fare.

BLONDIE AND THE OFFICE PLOT

The girls in the office found out that their boss,
a woman, left always at three.
They one day decided to do the same thing
and hoped that the boss wouldn't see.

When Blondie got home, she believed she could hear
the sounds of a love-making pair.
She peeked in the bedroom and saw with surprise
her husband and boss lying there.

A couple days later, when Blondie was asked
to join with the girls in their plot,
she turned down their offer and timidly said:
"The last time I nearly got caught!"

BLONDIE AND THE PAJAMAS

She learned to sew just recently.
She wished to do her part
to help the soldiers overseas.
Pajamas were her start.

She handed in a dozen pairs.
The major said, "No way.
You need to make a minor change,
and then they'll be okay."

"Pajamas need a fly," he said,
then bring them back again."
"You're wrong," said Blondie with a smile,
"they're not for married men."

BLONDIE AND THE PAPAL ELECTION

Blondie, a foe of corruption and graft,
was standing in St. Peter's square.
Waiting to learn of the cardinals' choice,
she hoped that the vote would be fair.

Watching the smokestack and hearing the name,
she voiced her disgust for the men.
"I knew it!" she yelled at the top of her lungs,
"they've chosen a Catholic again!"

BLONDIE AND THE PASTOR

She wrote a big check for the pastor one day

to pay for his basics, like bread.

She'd heard all the gossip from folks in the church:

"A very poor preacher," they said.

BLONDIE AND THE PHONE CALL

A misdialing caller woke Blondie one night;

he thought she'd be angry and groan.

"No problem," said Blondie, "I had to get up

and anyway answer the phone."

BLONDIE AND THE PHONE LIST

When listing numbers for the class,

she seemed to do just fine

until she went off-track again

and phoned to ask me mine.

BLONDIE AND THE POSTAGE STAMPS

With overblown frugality,

she thinks she should be praised

for buying lots of postage stamps

before the rates were raised.

BLONDIE AND THE PREGNANCY TEST

She's gaily telling all her friends
that she's expecting two.
She bought a box of home-kit strips;
the first one tested TRUE.

She tried another strip and found
the same result, same day,
which proved for her beyond a doubt
that twins are on the way.

BLONDIE AND THE REAL ESTATE AGENT

"I think I'll buy this hilltop house,"
said Blondie one fine day.
"I've got a question first to ask:
the sun comes up which way?"

The agent, shaken, said, "The East"
and planned to end the chat.
But Blondie gave a quick excuse,
"I don't keep up with that."

BLONDIE AND THE RECIPE

When Blondie faxed the recipe,

she had an afterthought.

She phoned her friend to send it back:

"For this is all I've got."

BLONDIE AND THE SCARF

The salesclerk was incredulous

as Blondie told her plight.

She wanted to return a scarf

which was, she said, too tight.

BLONDIE AND THE SECURITY CHECKS

"The staff will be given," the manager said,

"security checks any day."

"I'm thrilled," replied Blondie, "it surely will help

to supplement regular pay."

BLONDIE'S BOARDINGHOUSE

When Blondie smelled the kitchen gas,
she rushed and then was seething.
A boarder's head was in the stove
and he was deeply breathing.

"Now stop!" said Blondie angrily.
"You must have been deluded.
Our rule is kitchen privileges
have never been included."

BLONDIE AND THE SLIMMING CLUB

When Blondie quit the slimming club,

she shed a bitter tear.

She said, when asked how much she'd lost,

"A thousand bucks a year!"

BLONDIE AND THE SPELLING AWARD

She gave the boy a present;

he'd aced the spelling test.

The plaque had Blondie's wording,

proclaiming YOUR THE BEST.

BLONDIE AND THE STREET REPAIR

The diggers left a deep and wide –
but unprotected – hole.
So Blondie, hating ugliness,
fulfilled her civic role.

She hoped to please her driver friends,
who liked to see things neat.
She bought a tarp and fully hid
that portion of the street.

BLONDIE AND THE SUN LANDING

Blondie wrote the president:
"Have something great be done!
Show our might and expertise
and land men on the sun."

"Never!" was the strong response.
"They'd die from heat and light."
"Not a problem," Blondie said,
"they'd land there in the night."

BLONDIE AND THE TIGER

She liked the jaunty tiger
on a box that caught her eye.
A jigsaw fan, she bought it
and could hardly wait to try.

She emptied out the carton
but was stymied how to play.
She angrily and quickly
threw the Frosted Flakes away.

BLONDIE AND THE TITHE

She gives a tithe and finds it good,

a tenth for God's work here.

She plans to double that amount:

a twentieth next year.

BLONDIE AND THE TRAVEL AGENT

She claims the travel agent flirts;

he argues that's not true.

He says he's touting scenic sites,

and one's called "Isle of View."

BLONDIE AND THE VOCABULARY QUIZ

The teacher asked, "What's **paradox**?

Define it, Blondie, please."

"That's easy," was the fast reply.

"It's **man and wife MD's**".

BLONDIE AND THE WATCH

When I come late to work each day,

my boss, who's very Scotch,

keeps asking me what time it is.

He needs to buy a watch!"

BLONDIE AND THE WINDOW BILL

The double-paned windows had long been installed,
but Blondie had not paid a dime.
She felt it unfair for the firm to send bills
and quoted its language each time.

"Your ads are explicit; I don't owe a cent.
The proof, if you need it, is here.
You promise the windows will help me to save:
THEY PAY FOR THEMSELVES IN A YEAR!"

BLONDIE AND THE WINDSHIELD-WIPER

Poor Blondie's in the history books:
"The windshield wiper-queen."
She knew it was important that
the windshield be kept clean.

The new device was later made
more practical by far
when someone changed the mounting to
the outside of the car.

BLONDIE AT THE CHURCH BAZAAR

She focused on a full-length gown
and found it quite enticing.
She waited till the half-time mark,
announcing lowered pricing.

And then she bargained long and hard,
enjoying such occasions.
She asked at last if now the price
included alterations.

BLONDIE AT THE CONCERT

She left the concert very sad,

not knowing of her blunder.

She'd tried all night to catch the eye

of guest-star Stevie Wonder.

BLONDIE AT THE GARAGE

When going for checkups, I'm on the alert.

The charges mount up; it's a crime.

But now I play "expert" and hold down the bill

for turn-signal fluid each time.

BLONDIE AT THE LIBRARY

"This book was boring," Blondie said,

"the worst I've read by far."

"Please put it back," the clerk replied,

"where all the phone books are."

BLONDIE AT THE MALL

She drove to the mall on a hot summer day
with Rover along for the ride.
She rolled down the window on leaving the car
to aid circulation inside.

She yelled very loudly, "Stay there and don't move,"
and walked on her way to the shop.
"It's much more effective," a bystander said,
"to put it in PARK when you stop."

BLONDIE AT THE POST OFFICE

The clerk asked Blondie, wanting stamps:
"So which denomination?"
But Blondie'd never heard those words
in such a situation.

She took advantage of the change
and found it really nifty.
She gladly stated her request:
"Episcopalian, fifty."

BLONDIE GOES HORSEBACK

She'd never ridden in her life
but found the thought appealing.
Her dream came true the special day
she acted on her feeling.

She saw a horse that seemed to be
awaiting its next rider.
She mounted, keeping well in check
the butterflies inside her.

The horse began a steady trot
that led to her undoing.
She slipped around and lost her grip,
which signaled trouble brewing.

She yelled and soon a Wal-Mart man
arrived at that disaster:
"If you're around this horse again,
I'll pull the plug much faster."

BLONDIE GOES ICE-FISHING

When Blondie decided to fish through the ice,
she bought both a footstool and pole.
She took all her gear and established herself
and started to work on a hole.

In resolute tones came a voice from above,
"No fish are here under the ice!"
She moved many yards in response to the man
and heard the same message now twice.

She changed once again, for the guidance was clear;
she asked if the voice was the Lord.
"That isn't the case, and you'd better get out.
I manage the rink here," he roared.

BLONDIE IN THE COMPUTER CHAT ROOM

She chatted with friends by computer one day,
when smoke from a short caught her eye.
It rose in great billows behind her machine.
She didn't, however, know why.

She sent an alert to her friends in the chat
to warn them of forthcoming doom:
"Get out," she implored, "while the going is good;
I think there's a fire in your room!"

BLONDIE IN THE HIMALAYAS

Blondie's Himalayan trip,

which many want to do,

failed, she said, to satisfy:

"The mountains spoiled the view."

BLONDIE IN THE PARKING LOT

She fumed because the doors were locked;
the key was still inside.
Her being stranded in the lot
again had stung her pride.

She swore she'd not forget the things
she'd failed that day to do.
In future, she'd remove the key
and close the windows, too.

BLONDIE IN THE PHOTO SHOP

Blondie was the darkroom clerk,

who hung these signs about:

"Close the door real tight each time.

Don't let the dark leak out."

BLONDIE IN THE PLANE

The flight attendant was upset
as Blondie left her seat
and moved to First without a qualm;
she found it quite a treat.

The flight attendant asked in vain
that Blondie heed her plea.
"I'm staying here," was Blondie's cry,
"My ticket's Nashville, see?"

But Blondie moved when next she heard
the flight attendant say:
"Economy is Nashville-bound,
but First won't land today."

BLONDIE IN THE RESTAURANT

She watched as an underworld figure had lunch.

He sat just a few yards away.

She said, as he left before getting his bill,

"It's proof now that crime doesn't pay!"

BLONDIE ON CRIME

Aghast at the scandals in business these days,

the cheating and auditing wrongs,

she urges that crime be returned to the streets:

"For that's where it really belongs."

BLONDIE ON "JEOPARDY"

A guest on "Jeopardy" one day,
she showed her common sense.
Her category DAILY ACTS
had failed to make her tense:

"A woman does this sitting down;
a man while standing up.
On three and only three, you know,
it's done by every pup."

She smiled while others, turning red,
stood mute behind their stands.
She pushed her buzzer, shouting out:
"It's WHAT IS SHAKING HANDS?"

BLONDIE ON THE LONDON BUS

She left the upper deck in haste

on getting quite a scare.

"Imagine what I saw," she said,

"there was no driver there."

BLONDIE RAISES HER BANNER

"Stop war"—"Stop crime"—"Stop child abuse"

are banners all should lift.

But Blondie, worrywart, campaigns:

"Stop continental drift."

BLONDIE THE CANDY-STRIPER

So strongly is she germ-averse
she couldn't be a sickroom nurse.

She chose instead to volunteer,
a candy-striper of good cheer.

She likes her message-center work,
displaying, though, a troubling quirk:

She'll touch no fax – so scared is she --
arriving from Pathology.

BLONDIE THE CHANNEL SWIMMER

Three women were swimming the Channel one day;
reporters were waiting in France.
A redhead, brunette, and a blonde had a race;
each hoped it would be her big chance.

The redhead was first to step onto the beach,
acclaimed by the newsmen all 'round.
They gave a big cheer when the pretty brunette
soon planted her feet on the ground.

A half a day later, then Blondie arrived,
adept at displaying her charms.
"The prize should be mine, for they cheated," she said,
"I saw they were using their arms."

BLONDIE THE COMPUTER CLERK

Which computer clerk is new,

the greenest you have seen?

Blondie is the only one

with white-out on her screen.

BLONDIE THE DEAF-CLASS TEACHER

Your deafness shouldn't stop you!

I've some help that you can get.

The syllabus is ready

on an audio-cassette.

BLONDIE THE DRIVER

When Blondie was stopped by a trooper one day,

she worried she'd be in a jam.

"Will tickets," she asked, "be a problem for me

when taking the driver's exam?"

BLONDIE THE HIGHWAY PAINTER

A blonde was hired to paint a line:
the middle of the road.
The first day out she met her goal;
her talent really showed.

The second day she painted less;
her boss was not amused.
He gave her, though, a second chance:
"Consider it excused."

She later painted almost zilch;
it worsened every day.
"The reason," Blondie said, "is this:
the pail's so far away."

BLONDIE THE HIGHWAY TROOPER

The fast-driving woman was pulled off the road;
the officer asked for I.D.
The driver, who saw she was stopped by a blonde,
was planning on going scot-free.

She handed a mirror she took from her purse
and smiled as the officer looked.
"I see you're a trooper," said Blondie amazed,
"I'm sorry you almost got booked."

BLONDIE THE READING-CLASS TEACHER

Can't read at all? Then join my class.

You'll soon be "in the know."

Just follow the instructions here

and sign your name below.

BLONDIE THE REFORMER

Blondie's worked hard to reform her new beau,

grateful to say on her knees:

"Would you believe his behavior has turned

three hundred sixty degrees!"

BLONDIE THE WAITRESS

Aware the newly seated couple,

being deaf, would need help fast,

she placed before them special menus,

Braille ones leaving them aghast.

BLONDIE TO HAWAII

Hawaii's attractive but also quite far;

you're paying a lot for the plane.

So Blondie proposes to fly to the Coast

and do the remainder by train.

BLONDIE VISITS A DUDE RANCH

"I'm paying a lot for this weekend," she said,

demanding her rights and much more.

"I want, for example, the very best horse

that's never been ridden before."

BLONDIE'S AILMENTS

She boasts of enduring much aching and pain

with trouble in every known part.

One's cautious in asking the state of her health:

an organ recital will start.

BLONDIE'S BIRTH DATE

"So what's your birth date?" asked the judge,
"it's something that we need."
"Then Blondie said, "May thirty-first,"
"a happy day indeed."

"We want the year," the judge replied,
"you miss the point, I fear."
But Blondie said, "It's simple, judge,
"the same day every year."

BLONDIE'S BOYFRIEND

The mother said, "Blondie,
I don't like your boyfriend:
a loner and loafer. And how!

"Not true," countered Blondie,
"he told me he's doing
community service right now."

BLONDIE'S DIET

Though terribly busy, I'm healthy;

my diet is thoughtfully planned.

I eat from the four basic food groups:

what's bottled, bagged, frozen, and canned.

BLONDIE'S DINNERS FOR TWO

Shocked when he saw that she'd gained very much,

the doctor announced with a groan:

"Dinners for two are conducive to health,

but not when you're eating alone!"

BLONDIE'S DOCTOR

She fantasizes he's a flirt,

which worsens her neuritis.

She blushed when he announced, "You've got

acute appendicitis."

BLONDIE'S EAR-PIERCING SALON

She knows that inconvenience

is something people hate.

Her advertising slogan

is "Ears pierced while you wait."

BLONDIE'S FRIENDS

Dear Blondie's on the chubby side;

she's sociable and merry.

To Sara Lee she introduced

her buddies, Ben and Jerry.

BLONDIE'S HOMETOWN

Its reputation needs a boost,

as shown by an inspection.

Velveeta in an upscale store

is in the Gourmet Section.

BLONDIE'S I.Q.

People question her I.Q.

with jibes and jokes aplenty.

Now she has a sharp retort:

"For sure it's 20/20."

BLONDIE'S INVITATION

When Blondie was riding the subway one day,
she talked to a Jesuit priest:
"I'd really be happy if you and your wife
could join me for coffee at least."

The priest was astonished: "We've CELIBACY.
I hope that means something to you."
"It does," answered Blondie. "Say Hi to your wife
and see that your youngster comes, too!"

BLONDIE'S LATENESS

She leisurely got to her workplace at ten;

the owner was fit to be tied.

"We missed you two hours ago, Blondie," he said.

"What happened at eight?" she replied.

BLONDIE'S LAWYER

She needs a good lawyer for help on her case

and chose one with ads on TV.

She has an appointment today at the firm;

it's Ketchum and Cheatham PC.

BLONDIE THE MANICURIST

An out-of-town fellow decided to stop
to splurge on a leisurely shave.
When Blondie, the manicure girl, touched his hand,
he quickly became very brave.

"So what do you say we have fun later on?"
The fellow asked, starting his plea.
"I can't," Blondie answered, "It's wrong and what's more,
my husband would kill me, you see."

"No problem, my dear, you'll be home in good time.
Your husband won't know what we've planned."
"He knows it already," then Blondie announced,
"The razor's right now in his hand."

BLONDIE'S LIBRARY WOES

She missed the due date once again

and once again must pay.

The title of her late return?

"Time Management Today."

BLONDIE'S MEDICAL ECONOMIES

She's planning to economize
on future doctor bills:
the cost of tests and surgery
and different colored pills.

When doctors' films show trouble spots,
she'll smile and act the tease.
She thinks they'll surely act when asked:
"Retouch the x-rays, please."

BLONDIE'S NEW THERMOMETER

She bought a new thermometer

a red-hot summer day.

She'd waited, for she thought she'd get

more mercury that way.

BLONDIE'S PLANE RESERVATION

The agent asked Blondie, "Your wishes?

A window perhaps? Do you care?"

"A seat on the aisle," she responded,

"I don't want the wind in my hair."

BLONDIE'S PUPS

Timex and Rolex are Blondie's new pups.

Her neighbors and friends are amazed.

Blondie's upset when they question the names.

"They're watch dogs," she answers unfazed.

BLONDIE'S RÉSUMÉ

Her résumé's a legend;

everything's sublime.

But something's clearly missing:

"Once upon a time."

BLONDIE'S REVENGE

She nursed a drink, relaxing
at a table in the bar.
She noticed she was clearly
being ogled from afar.

A man approached her suavely
and began to give his spiel:
"You're quite a looker, honey,
just for you I've got a deal.

"For twenty bucks you've got me
for whatever you may care.
And put your wish in writing,
so I'll know what I can dare."

With fear and trepidation,
she extended to the louse
the cash and slip of paper
which read simply: "Clean my house."

BLONDIE'S SIGN

She's ringing doorbells all day long

to sell her new creation.

A sign she says a house should have,

it's NO SOLICITATION.

BLONDIE'S SOLO FLIGHT

Her solo test lacked elegance;

the landing hurt her pride.

"The strip," she said, "was much too short

but very, very wide."

BLONDIE'S SPARTAN DIET

Some time ago I made a vow
and set the rule I follow now.
Just once a month I eat a sweet
and wouldn't ever stoop to cheat.

Obeying's hard, but I don't whine,
for character is on the line.
The date for cake I'm eating here
is April of the coming year.

BLONDIE'S SUPERMARKET JOB

A fellow asked for condiments

in Blondie's deli aisle.

She said with glee, "Try Pharmacy,"

and gave a knowing smile.

BLONDIE'S TRAFFIC VIOLATION

"Your problem is," His Honor said,
"a traffic violation.
You failed to heed a One-Way sign
and caused a situation."

Then Blondie said, "I had to make
a right-or-left selection.
But once I chose, I swear I drove
in only one direction."

BLONDIE'S TRAVEL PLANS

Since never being far from home,

she thinks what she should do

is go to France and Germany

and maybe Europe, too.

BLONDIE'S TREMORS

Her tremors are distressing

and she knows what makes her quake:

"Too often jars and bottles

have a label reading SHAKE."

Made in the USA
Middletown, DE
03 December 2022

16904910R00068